IF I COULD TAKE YOUR TEARS

Words and Photos by Mary Lou Moran

MARY LOU MORAN

If I could Take Your Tears – Echoes of Domestic Violence
First edition, published 2018

By Mary Lou Moran
Author Photo: Clayton Beck Photography
Styling: Isha Casagrande Styling
Photographs provided by Mary Lou Moran

Copyright © 2018, Mary Lou Mickel

Hardbound ISBN-13: 978-1-942661-94-8

All rights reserved. No part of this book may be reproduced or transmitted in any form or by any means, electronic or mechanical, including photocopying, recording or by any information storage and retrieval system, without written permission from the author, except for the inclusion of brief quotations in a review.

Published by Kitsap Publishing
P.O. Box 572
Poulsbo, WA 98370
www.KitsapPublishing.com

150-10 9 8 7 6 5 4 3 2 1

My Words are offered wholly and earnestly to anyone who has been treated in a harmful, hurtful way in the hope that you, too, can realize your value and find your voice.

Mary Lou Moran

Off in the distance

She's painting with words

Eyes open

Then closing

Designing

Brush in motion

Letters arrive

Words gather

Some thrive

Hands move hastily

To capture them all

Some are relinquished

Where do they fall

Out on the edge

Ready to fly

Can't get the wind up

I don't know why

One small breeze

Surely will make me let go

Once in midair

Can I handle the flow

Moments of madness

Moments of despair

How long do I stay there

I ride like a bird

On the edge of a cloud

Wings barely flapping

Afraid to come down

I am like a child in my sweet sleep Reaching for the stars

Not afraid to fall down

Dreams have endings and they are not for keeps

Chilled inside

Barely alive

Pushing up

To light

Still inside

Almost breaking out

Feeling strength

Slowly Leading out

One final burst

Spring is born

If only

I could stop the love I have for you

Maybe I could begin to live my life through

You cause my heart to cry

My mind to wander

With each time I see you leave

A part of me dies

I thought myself not strong enough

To hold myself alone

Now I see I haven't been holding only me

The strings are almost free

Beginning to untwine

Though frayed and thin and surely broke

I know I can count on those lines

The load has now lightened

Strings time to mend

And once around this corner

They'll hold me up again

Voices are calling

Strangers to my mind

Voices whispering

Seem to know my name

Echoes sound through my brain

Can't find escape

Open the door

Be free, be me

Open the door

The little voice said

Let the light in

Said the man in my head

Swiftly flowing

Slowly going away

Floating out

From flesh and bone

Soul remains

Taking the journey

Away from it all

Alone

On my own

Hiding inside fear

Cheated by words

That were lies

Threatened by words

That weren't

Scared to try

Let someone inside

Baring all

May be for nothing

Can you see me?

I am still here

The same

Have not changed

Where did you go?

Is it far away?

It is okay

I understand

This is not a wonderland

In a time where pain lived

Emptiness ruled

Walls built high

No door to escape

Or enter

Dark loneliness

Looms brightly

Inside

Small flickers

Of love

Burned space

Through Somewhere inside

A place in me is suspended there

Go inside to that place

Where the dark is close

Holds your soul

Go in deeper

Do not come out

Sink to the floor

No escape or door

Drink from the well

That flows from hell

Til you're so full

You don't care

Where you are anymore

Close the hatch

Tighten it down

Don't let anyone around

She is still watching
Holding on
Mostly silent now
She rests in the corner
Of my heart
Still holds the strings
To some actions
All precautionary
She protects me
She thinks
She knows I am stronger
For so long she was my strength
My alarm to hide
My feet to dig in
My flight from any source of pain or uncertainty
We struggle now together
Her & I
I feel her hand stroking my hair
Wiping tears from eyes held tight
Telling me she is there
As always
Watching

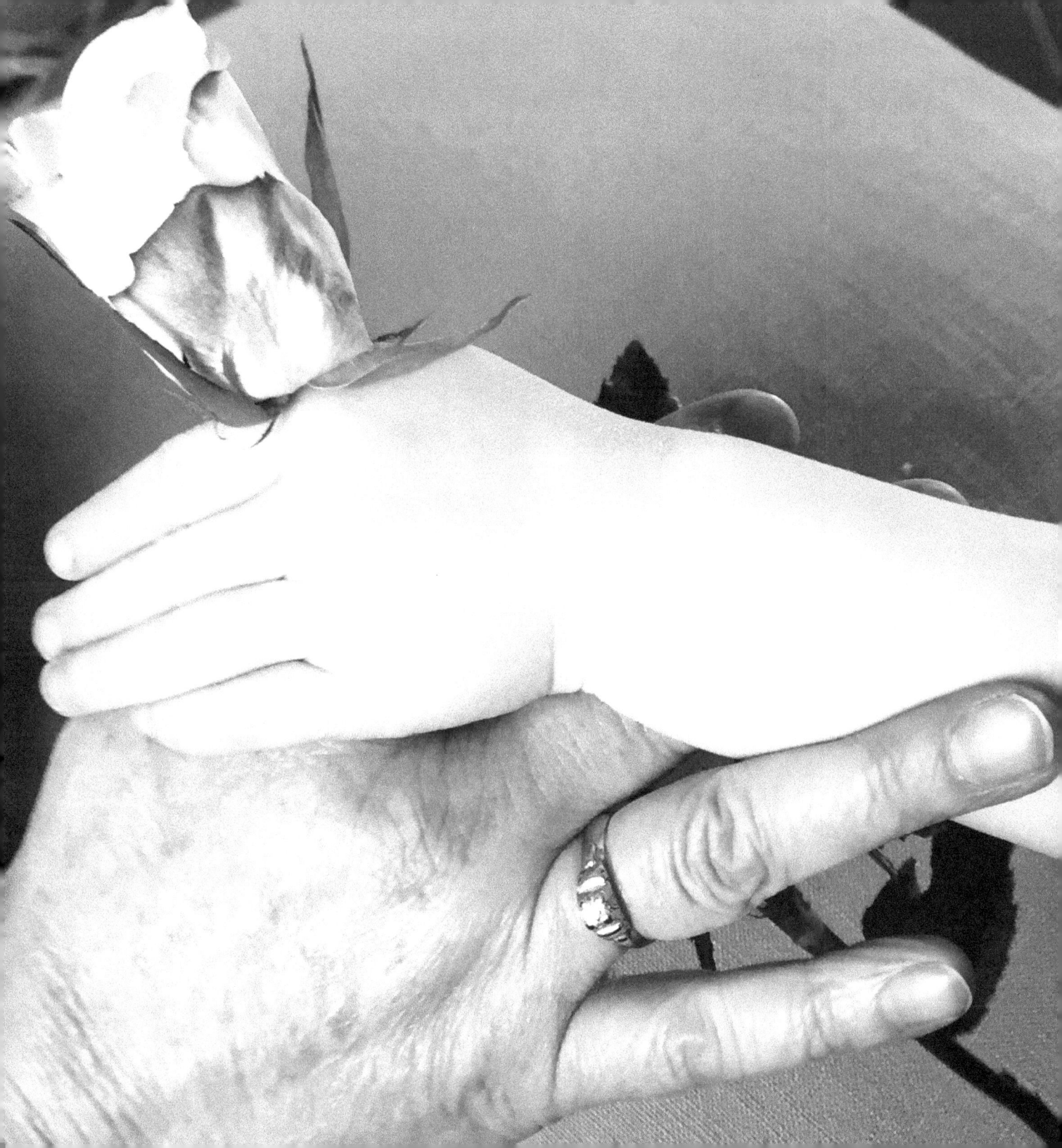

She is sleeping

Her head rests lightly On my lap

Her breathing calm Not frantic

Not racing

With old worry

Her face holds

A new & surprising peace

Her muscles relax

Her skin illuminates

A contented softness

She dreams of

Trickling water

Falling sweetly

Onto polished stones

Water shines them

As if treasured gold

Of lavendar fields

A colorful carpet

Heavenly scented

Only for her

Of indigo skies

High over her head

Cotton clouds

Arranged for her imagination

Of love

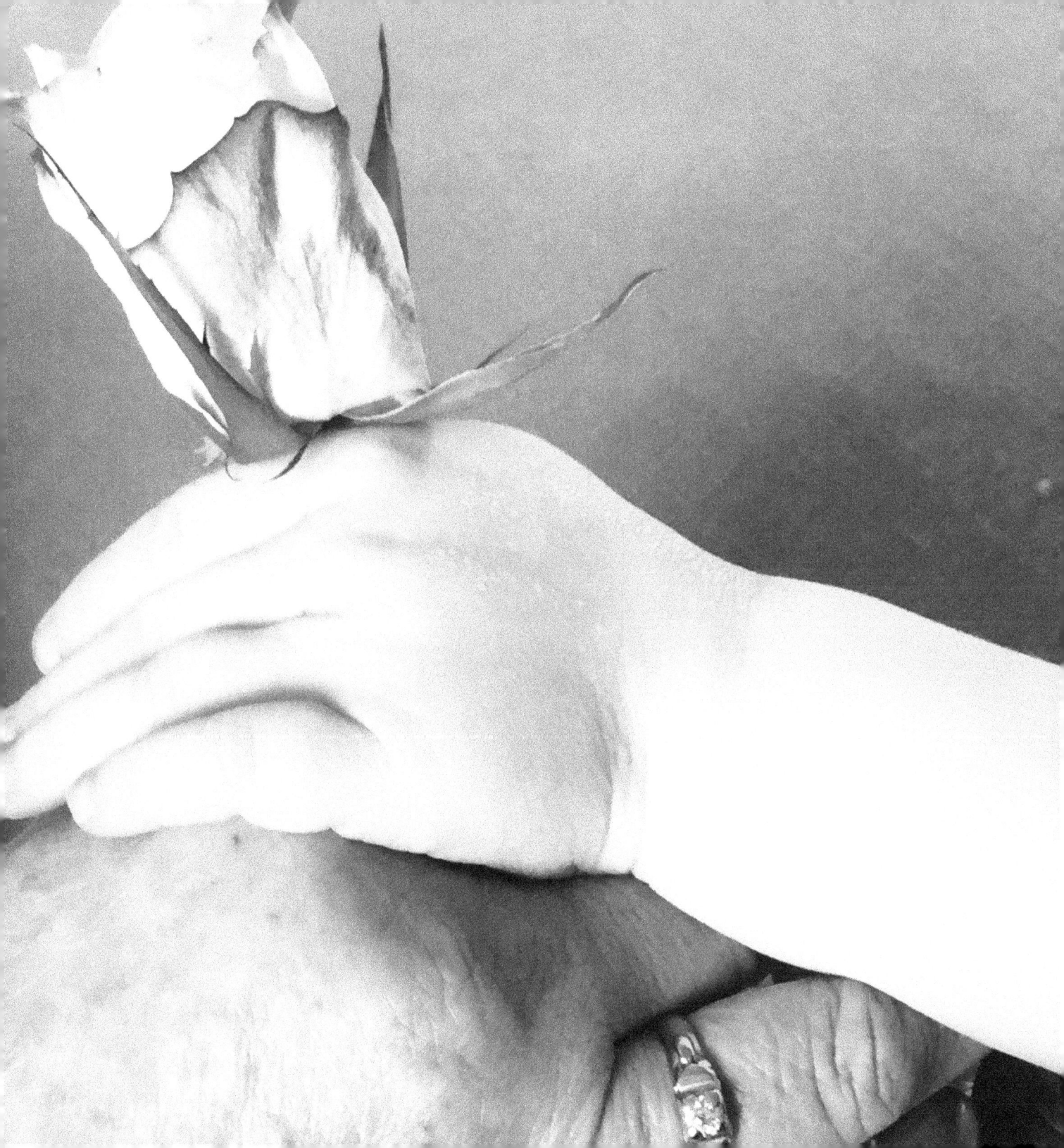

She's been sleeping for quite some time now

The book I read woke her

She's become her old self

Pulling on me

Trying hard to close the door

I opened in my heart for him

She's yelling you should know better

Leaving places exposed

Pain slips in

Unnoticed

She's angry & tired

Of protecting

My mind is numb

Thoughts swirl

Melting my strength

Sleep is relief

Her words quieted there

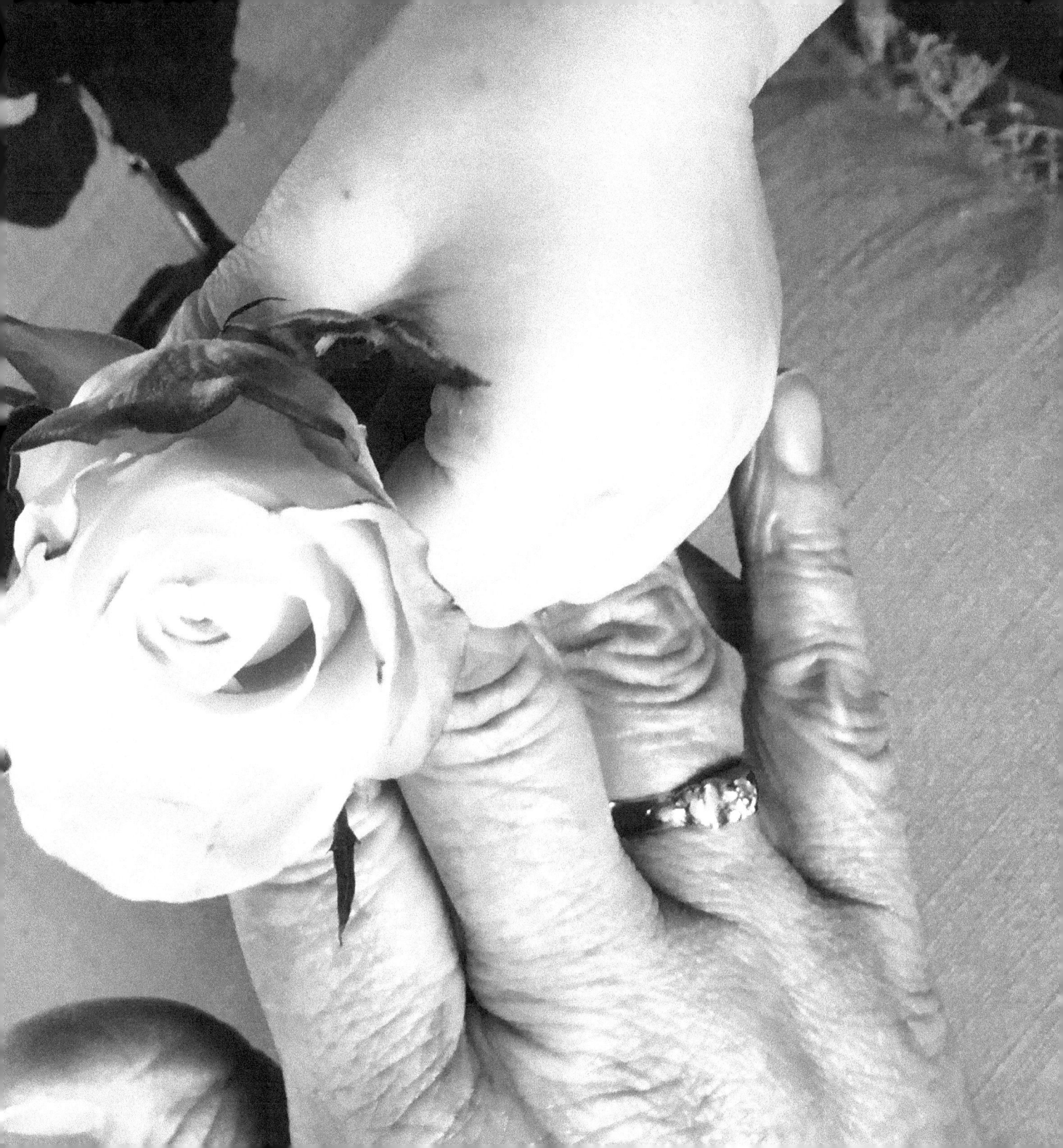

I thought you took all of me
Away with your shame
But just take a look
I'm still here I'm still me
Can you remember the feelings when you took your fist
Did you realize then what it would do to me
Was there relief inside when your anger was spent
Did you notice the pieces down by your feet
But just take a look
I'm still here I'm still me
I know you damaged yourself just as much as me
You tried so long to transfer that pain
I hope inside you it doesn't remain
No matter how hard you try
I will always fight back
Just take a look
I'm still here I'm still me
I hope you've found peace
I hope your rage sleeps
I hope your hands fall softly
On love some day
So just take a look
I'm still here I'm still me

She's there

Holding on

Her small hand in mine

The other gently brushing

Her hair to the side

She looks tentatively forward

Carefully glancing around

I fill with ease

She leans on me now

My arms close around her tiny frame

She melts into me

Quiets her tears

She knows from my whispers

Her need almost gone

She'll be with me always

As if an old song

She'll dance in my spirit

And sing in my soul

She is detached

From the gray dark hollow

She only knew

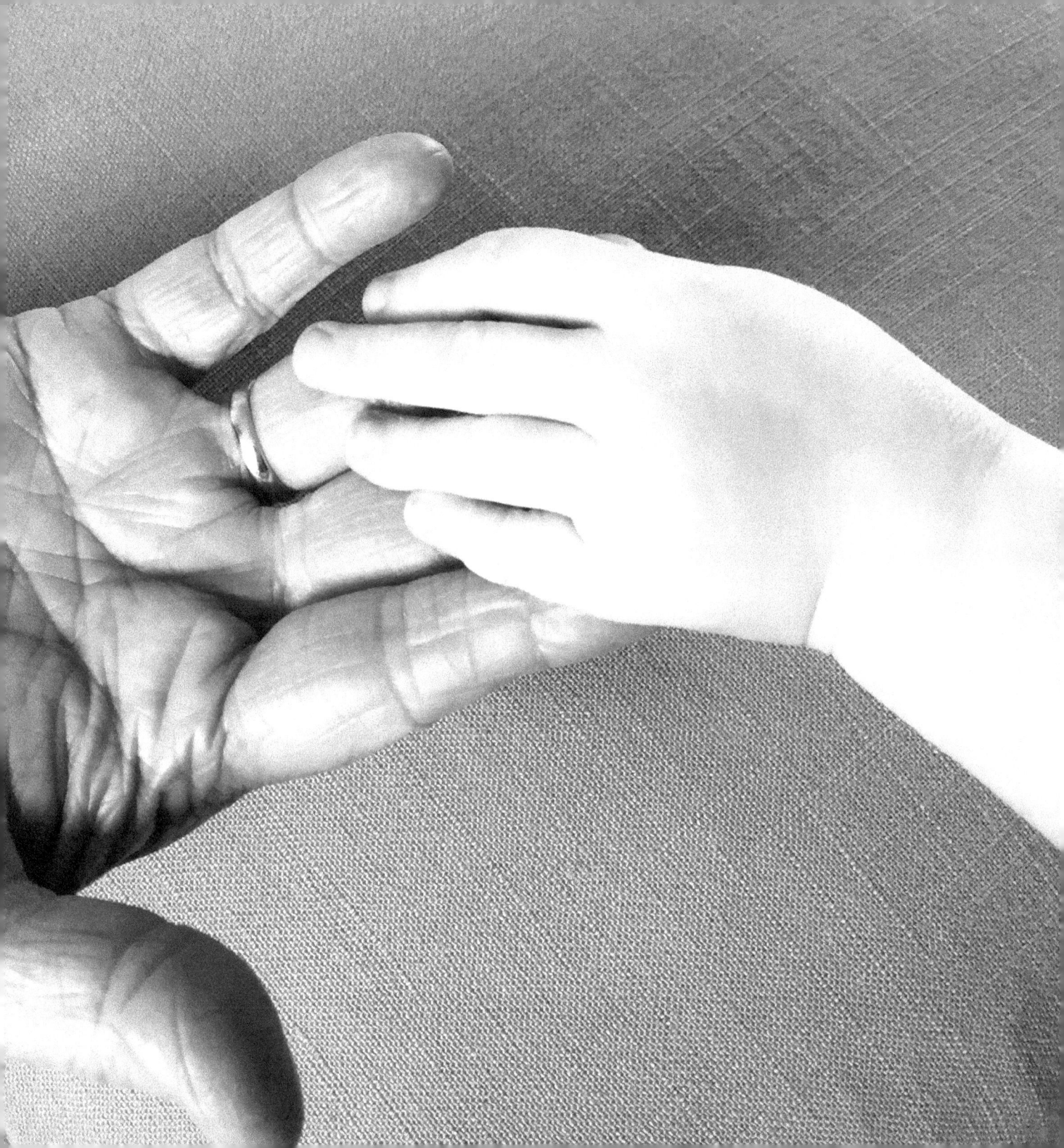

Fragile spirit acting like steel

Crystals clustered

Flowing through

Jagged edges

True & kind

Tough your soul

The fire lights

In bleeding heart

Pieces crumble never fail

Icy spears

Illuminating shards of light

Melts the fear & leaves what's right

He said to look outside

Capture a picture

Something pretty

Something free

A carpet of green

All around me

Tightly woven

Together bound

Leaves intertwine

No separation found

Traveling downward

They whisper thru

Tiny bell flowers

Twinkling blue

I see him

In the wind he blows

In the stars he shines

He's there in mountains & valleys

He artfully drew

In the birds that soar

In the sky he bore

The sun his warmth

On every day

Dark night

His comfort

Dream away

The moon his night light

Til morning does rise

He's always there

Just open your eyes

You'll see innocence

And wonder inside

All His creations

February 26, 2018

I slept with my poems last night

Brought back the fear and flight

Long ago pain

Composed in black

Carassed me

Moments stood still

Heaviness faded

Until only white

Lay beside me